MW00907478

COGAT
GRADE 1-3

Copyright © 2024 by Mirvoxid Press

All rights reserved.

No portion of this book may be reproduced in any form without written permission from the publisher or author.

This publication is designed to provide accurate and authoritative information in regard to the subject matter covered. It is sold with the understanding that neither the author nor the publisher is engaged in rendering legal, investment, accounting or other professional services. While the publisher and author have used their best efforts in preparing this book, they make no representations or warranties with respect to the accuracy or completeness of the contents of this book and specifically disclaim any implied warranties of merchantability or fitness for a particular purpose. No warranty may be created or extended by sales representatives or written sales materials. The advice and strategies contained herein may not be suitable for your situation. You should consult with a professional when appropriate. Neither the publisher nor the author shall be liable for any loss of profit or any other commercial damages, including but not limited to special, incidental, consequential, personal, or other damages.

Cover by Mirvoxid Press
Illustrations by Mirvoxid Press

Content:

Overview of *CogAT* for Parents
What is the *Cognitive Abilities Test™* (*CogAT®*)?

The term "cognitive ability" describes a student's capacity to learn in a variety of contexts and settings and exhibit original problem-solving techniques. A child's ability to reason abstractly and recognize patterns and correlations in their environment is measured by the Cognitive Abilities Test (CogAT), as opposed to a typical achievement test, which gauges how well a student has mastered the curriculum.

Verbal, nonverbal, and quantitative reasoning are the three domains, or batteries, in which the CogAT assesses reasoning. These domains are based on the key ways that students and teachers interact in the classroom. The kinds of items contained in each CogAT battery are depicted in Figure 1. A representative item from each subtest (second grade level) is displayed in Figure 2.

Figure 1

Types of Reasoning Assessed

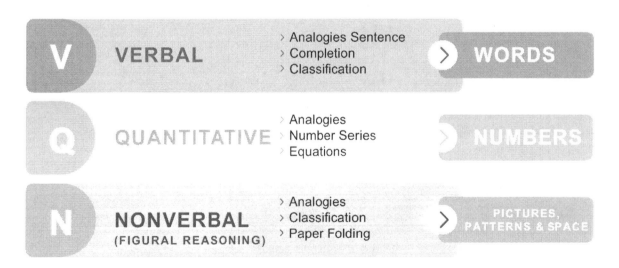

Figure 2

Verbal – Picture Analogies

Verbal – Picture Classification

Verbal – Sentence Completion (not pictured)

Figure 2   *Continued*

Quantitative – Number Analogies

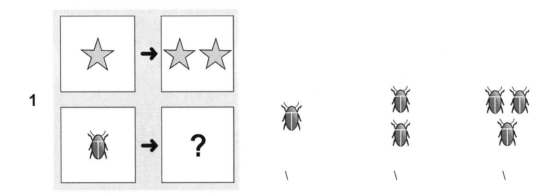

1

Quantitative – Number Puzzles

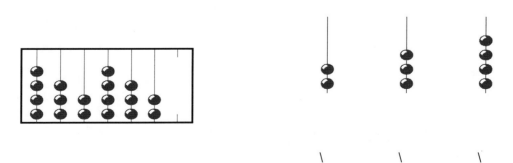

| 2 | 3 | 4 | 6 |

\   \   \   \

Quantitative – Number Series

Figure 2 *Continued*

Nonverbal – Figure Matrices

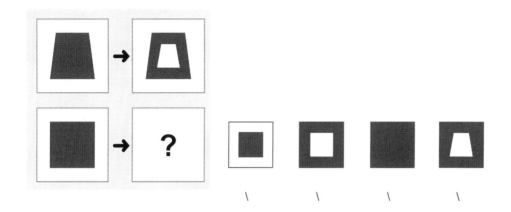

Nonverbal – Figure Classification

Nonverbal – Paper Folding

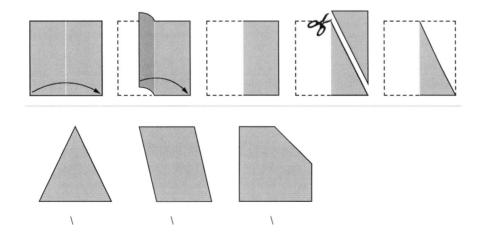

Each student obtains an Ability Profile—a brief code that encapsulates their cognitive abilities—after completing the entire CogAT. This guide will help you comprehend ability data and how to use it, as well as how to interpret the Ability Profile.

Interpreting the *Ability Profile*

An Ability Profile code similar to this one is awarded to each student who completes the required amount of items on the entire CogAT:

8   B   (Q-)

LEVEL   PATTERN   STRENGTH/WEAKNESS

With the use of this Ability Profile, educators may better cater to the requirements of their students, help parents better support their kids at home, and provide students a deeper grasp of their own learning. The interpretation of each section of the profile is explained in the following sections.

Level

The student's median age represented by a number appears at the beginning of each CogAT Ability Profile. In comparison to other pupils of the same age, this shows the student's general degree of thinking ability. "Standard nine" is shortened to "stanine." The fact that stanine scores vary from a low of 1 to a high of 9 is where the name originates.

Interpreting Stanine Level

Level	Indication
1, 2, 3	below average
4, 5, 6	average
7, 8	above average
9	very high

The test computes scores using a national sample of test results, referred to as "national norms". Students between the ages of four years and eleven months and eighteen and over are grouped by age every month. Your child performed at around the same level as other pupils their age who took the test, according to the test results if they received an average stanine score (4-6). A youngster outperformed other test-takers if they receive a stanine score of seven or above, which is above average. A child's performance on the exam was poorer than that of other pupils their age if their stanine score was below average (1-3). For a graphic illustration, see to Figure 3:

Figure 3

Median Stanine by Reasoning Ability Level

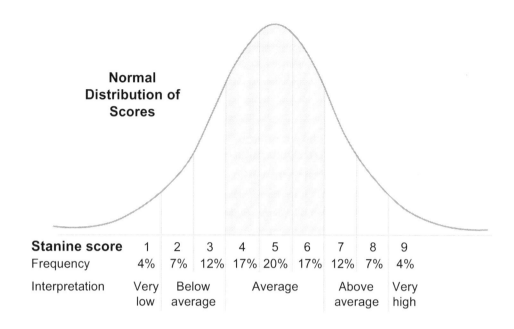

Stanine score	1	2	3	4	5	6	7	8	9
Frequency	4%	7%	12%	17%	20%	17%	12%	7%	4%
Interpretation	Very low	Below average		Average			Above average		Very high

Pattern

A letter that represents the scoring pattern for your child comes after the median score. The pattern indicates whether there is a substantial difference in some of the three battery results or whether they are all roughly equal. A, B, C, or E profiles can be applied to the pattern.

Pattern	Description	Approximate percentage of students with this profile
A	The student's Verbal, Quantitative, and Nonverbal Battery scores are roughly at the sAme level	44%
B	Two of the scores are roughly the same. The third score is a relative strength or weakness, significantly aBove or Below the other two.	33%
C	Two scores Contrast. The student shows a relative strength and a relative weakness.	12%
E	An E profile indicates Extreme score differences. At least two scores differ by 24 or more points on the standard age score (SAS) scale.	10%

Relative strengths and weaknesses

Following the pattern, there might be one or two more letters that represent the student's relative strengths and/or weaknesses as shown by their battery scores, depending on their Ability Profile. Remember that these are just related to the child's other skills, not the skills of other pupils. Not every profile has these extra characters. Here's how to read these letters, for those who do:

- V, Q, or N followed by a plus sign (+) indicates a relative strength on the Verbal, Quantitative, or Nonverbal Battery, respectively.

- V, Q, or N followed by a minus sign (–) indicates a relative weakness on the Verbal, Quantitative, or Nonverbal Battery, respectively.

Sample score interpretations

A student with an Ability Profile of 4B (V+) has an average median score of 4, and their Verbal Battery result was significantly higher (above) than their scores on the other two batteries. Here are some more illustrations of profiles and how they should be interpreted:

Profile	Interpretation
9A	Very high scores on all three batteries
8B (Q-)	Generally high scores but a relative weakness on the Quantitative Battery
2B (N+)	Generally below average scores, but a relative strength on the Nonverbal Battery
5C (V+N-)	Generally average scores with a relative strength on the Verbal Battery and a relative weakness on the Nonverbal Battery
8E (V-)	Generally high scores but an extreme relative weakness on the Verbal Battery

How can ability data **be used**?

A special and effective tool that tells parents, teachers, and students about a student's potential is the Ability Profile.

Teachers can arrange students with people who will complement and enhance their learning and modify lessons based on best practices for each ability level using the information from the profile. To promote academic progress, teachers can also employ focused techniques to build on pupils' unique strengths and help them strengthen their weaknesses. Students who are relatively strong in verbal reasoning, for instance, will gain from discussing or writing about what they are learning, whereas students who are stronger in nonverbal reasoning will gain from learning new concepts through the use of models and manipulatives. Rather than expecting a student who struggles with verbal reasoning to remember instructions, it could be more advantageous to write instructions on the board for them to refer to. When explaining math issues to a student who struggles with quantitative thinking, it is usually best to use illustrations and/or written explanations.

As parents, we can utilize this knowledge to help our kids learn and develop their critical thinking abilities at home. To make the most of the Ability Profile data, we invite you to review the Additional Resources listed below.

An important note about test scores

You child is a one-of-a-kind person with many incomparable personal traits and qualities that will shape what they bring to the world. You should know that the CogAT is just one test, and that results can be different based on many outside factors. It is still a great way to find out what our students are capable of. These results are a great way to see how well a student is doing in school, but they are not the only way to judge your child's skills and abilities. The school for your child uses a variety of tests, data, and notes to figure out what they need. If you want to help your child learn and reach their full potential, we hope that the Ability Profile will be useful to you and their teacher.

Verbal Reasoning

This question needs one letter to fit in both sets of boxes.
This letter will finish the word before the box and start the word after the box for both sets.
Click on the right answer from the list of five.

1)	R	I	D	☐	D	I	T		T	A	K	☐	V	I	L
2)	B	O	L	☐	R	A	M		M	E	L	☐	U	R	N
3)	C	O	P	☐	E	A	R		O	N	L	☐	A	R	D
4)	L	U	C	☐	N	E	W		B	A	N	☐	I	N	G
5)	H	I	G	☐	U	G	E		S	U	C	☐	A	L	F
6)	F	I	L	☐	O	O	N		F	A	R	☐	E	A	T
7)	F	L	O	☐	A	I	T		S	N	O	☐	I	S	H
8)	T	O	U	☐	E	N	T		P	A	I	☐	E	A	D
9)	L	O	G	☐	K	A	Y		O	N	T	☐	P	E	N
10)	C	L	U	☐	O	N	D		B	U	L	☐	O	O	K

1)	O ☐	A ☐	E ☐	U ☐	I ☐
2)	D ☐	T ☐	B ☐	O ☐	Y ☐
3)	E ☐	H ☐	N ☐	Y ☐	C ☐
4)	Y ☐	D ☐	R ☐	S ☐	K ☐
5)	H ☐	K ☐	C ☐	G ☐	L ☐
6)	O ☐	N ☐	M ☐	H ☐	S ☐
7)	W ☐	B ☐	F ☐	D ☐	P ☐
8)	M ☐	R ☐	N ☐	B ☐	D ☐
9)	A ☐	I ☐	U ☐	E ☐	O ☐
10)	P ☐	N ☐	L ☐	B ☐	C ☐

To make two new 4-letter words, one letter needs to be taken out of the first 5-letter word and added to the second 3-letter word.
You can't change the order of the letters.

			1st New Word	2nd New Word
1)	table	hat		
2)	chant	sad		
3)	bring	all		
4)	could	for		
5)	given	had		
6)	crave	fog		
7)	drive	tip		
8)	swing	tin		
9)	learn	pay		
10)	along	try		
11)	house	sit		
12)	sport	was		
13)	solid	pad		
14)	beard	own		
15)	shock	owl		

13

Find the word that both sets of words mean at the same time.

1)   (bird, fowl)   (bend, dodge)

2)   (holiday, journey)   (fall, stumble)

3)   (tool, equipment)   (observed, spotted)

4)   (branch, stem)   (follow, hunt)

5)   (sphere, orb)   (dance, event)

6)   (type, variety)   (nice, thoughtful)

7)   (remaining, left)   (relax, sleep)

8)   (vehicle, transport)   (study, prepare)

9)   (cold, chilly)   (trendy, fashionable)

10)   (rest, pause)   (fracture, shatter)

1. avoid ☐	animal ☐	move ☐	duck ☐	miss ☐
2. trip ☐	vacation ☐	falter ☐	slip ☐	ramble ☐
3. apparatus ☐	saw ☐	noticed ☐	view ☐	machine ☐
4. track ☐	offshoot ☐	stalk ☐	look ☐	twig ☐
5. ball ☐	disco ☐	circle ☐	celebration ☐	round ☐
6. pleasant ☐	agreeable ☐	group ☐	kind ☐	sort ☐
7. nap ☐	leftover ☐	rest ☐	spare ☐	excess ☐
8. improve ☐	train ☐	move ☐	learn ☐	car ☐
9. cool ☐	sharp ☐	popular ☐	fresh ☐	crisp ☐
10. sever ☐	split ☐	stop ☐	break ☐	cease ☐

Check each sentence to see if you can find a four-letter word that is hidden between two other words. The words will always be next to each other.

Example

The black bat hid in the cave.

Answer

The black **bat h**id in the cave.

bath

Sentence		Hidden Word
1)	The children wear hats and gloves in winter.	⟶	
2)	The birds often made their nests in the tree.	⟶	
3)	The hungry bear chose to eat the sweet honey.	⟶	
4)	They whispered the secret plan excitedly to each other.	⟶	
5)	The watchful hare stopped and waited in the field.	⟶	
6)	The team asked who would be playing in the game.	⟶	
7)	The full moon cast a deep shadow nearby.	⟶	
8)	The tadpole begins to wriggle and swims away.	⟶	
9)	She went to play in the park with her dog.	⟶	
10)	The old dragon emerged from the dark cave.	⟶	

This alphabet will help you figure out each question's answer.

For each question, you will need to come up with a different code.

A B C D E F G H I J K L M N O P Q R S T U V W X Y Z

Example

If the code for BOX is CPY, what is IBU the code for?

Answer

HAT

Answer

1) If the code for HOUSE is KRXVH, what does JDUGHQ mean?

2) If the code for SHIP is XMNU, what is the code for TRAIN?

3) If the code for GREEN is FQDDM, what does XDKKNV mean?

4) If the code for LION is MHPM, what is the code for BEAR?

5) If the code for JUMPER is LWORGT, what does VTQWUGTU mean?

6) If the code for THUNDER is QERKABO, what is the code for SUNSHINE?

7) If the code for HAND is LERH, what does JSSX mean?

8) If the code for PENCIL is VKTIOR, what is the code for PAINT?

9) If the code for MOON is OMQL, what does URCP mean?

10) If the code for CHERRY is EIGSTZ, what is the code for BANANA?

Pick two words, one from each group, that will form a new correct word when joined together. In the answer, the word from the first group will always come first.

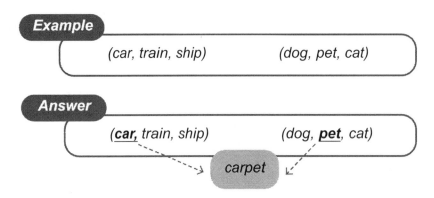

Example

(car, train, ship)   (dog, pet, cat)

Answer

(**car,** train, ship)   (dog, **pet**, cat)

carpet

Answer

1)   (bridge, dam, road)   (old, young, age)

2)   (steam, air, water)   (fall, trip, stumble)

3)   (power, energy, battery)   (more, less, equal)

4)   (day, month, week)   (cease, finish, end)

5)   (there, is, are)   (rock, sky, land)

6)   (sea, wave, surf)   (mother, daughter, son)

7)   (yes, no, maybe)   (body, foot, head)

8)   (rot, break, age)   (eight, nine, ten)

9)   (out, in, near)   (fold, crease, bend)

10) (trousers, jacket, suit)   (sack, box, case)

Pick the two words from each group that mean the same thing:

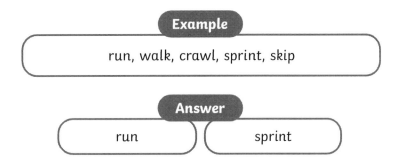

Example

run, walk, crawl, sprint, skip

Answer

| run | sprint |

Answer

1) tiny, huge, round, medium, enormous

2) warm, umbrella, cold, freezing, raining

3) far, near, sky, distant, mountain

4) wide, short, thin, tall, narrow

5) dirty, wash, scrub, bubbles, water

6) start, lose, begin, win, race

7) awake, sleep, bed, snooze, pyjamas

8) plate, spoon, cup, teapot, mug

9) happy, bored, joyous, party, sad

10) sea, wave, boat, sail, yacht

Letters stand in for numbers in this game.

Do the math and fill in the blanks with the right letters for each answer.

Example

If A = 13, B = 5, C = 15, D= 3 and E = 12, what is the answer to this sum written as a letter?

C - B + D = ?

Answer

C (15) - B (5) = 10, 10 + D (3) = 13

The answer is A, as A = 13

		Sum	Answer
1)	If A = 7, B = 9, C = 15, D = 16 and E = 14, what is the answer to the sum written as a letter?	E + B - A =	
2)	If A = 9, B = 11, C = 16, D = 4 and E = 7, what is the answer to the sum written as a letter?	D + C - B =	
3)	If A = 4, B = 12, C = 9, D = 17 and E = 8, what is the answer to the sum written as a letter?	D - B + A =	
4)	If A = 6, B = 10, C = 9, D = 7 and E = 11, what is the answer to the sum written as a letter?	E + A - D =	
5)	If A = 15, B = 6, C = 18, D = 7 and E = 17, what is the answer to the sum written as a letter?	C - D + B =	
6)	If A = 23, B = 4, C = 16, D = 11 and E = 13, what is the answer to the sum written as a letter?	A + B - C =	
7)	If A = 17, B = 19, C = 26, D = 31 and E = 12, what is the answer to the sum written as a letter?	D - A + E =	
8)	If A = 18, B = 43, C = 49, D = 29 and E = 54, what is the answer to the sum written as a letter?	B + D - A =	
9)	If A = 28, B = 24, C = 9, D = 26 and E = 5, what is the answer to the sum written as a letter?	A - C + E =	
10)	If A = 18, B = 16, C = 19, D = 20 and E = 17, what is the answer to the sum written as a letter?	C + E - B =	

19

Pick two words, one from each group, that mean the exact opposite of each other.

Example

(under, low, floor)   (wall, beside, over)

Answer

under   over

Answer

1) (time, before, morning)   (after, late, waiting)

2) (pebble, stone, blunt)   (soil, sharp, beach)

3) (smooth, perfect, even)   (number, odd, unique)

4) (slow, competition, walk)   (rush, hurry, fast)

5) (bottle, full, bag)   (empty, eaten, meal)

6) (above, high, ceiling)   (ground, below, down)

7) (enquire, talk, question)   (tell, speak, answer)

8) (arrival, holiday, airport)   (home, departure, late)

9) (dream, asleep, blanket)   (awake, day, school)

10) (create, draw, paint)   (messy, untidy, destroy)

Pick two words that need to move around in the sentence for it to make sense.

Example

The night rode out into the knight.

knight   night

Answer

The **knight** rode out into the **night**.

Answer

1) The squirrel buried the tree under the acorn.

2) Have your brushed you teeth today?

3) The sandy waves crashed onto the rough shore.

4) She blew out the cake on her birthday candles.

5) The morning clock rang early in the alarm.

6) The pool is wear we where our swimming costumes.

7) The sky shone in the night stars.

8) The Christmas children opened their excited presents.

9) When it is cold, their put they coats on.

10) Are favourite colours our red and blue.

Three of the words in each group go together. Which two words don't go with the other three?

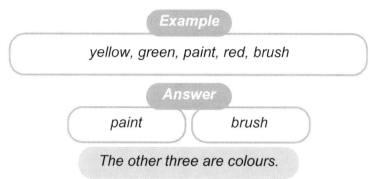

Example

yellow, green, paint, red, brush

Answer

paint   brush

The other three are colours.

Answer

1) train, ship, boat, lorry, yacht

2) elephant, fish, shark, dolphin, giraffe

3) oak, daisy, willow, daffodil, birch

4) cat, pigeon, dog, parrot, eagle

5) horse, beetle, ant, hamster, centipede

6) cold, hat, gloves, snow, scarf

7) gale, hurricane, sun, cyclone, rainbow

8) cry, laugh, weep, chuckle, giggle

9) pencil, paper, pen, notebook, biro

10) amble, rush, hurry, saunter, dash

Each group has two words that should be checked off to finish the sentence.

1) Strawberry is to
   - juicy ☐
   - fruit ☐
   - red ☐

   as carrot is to
   - vegetable ☐
   - ground ☐
   - rabbit ☐

2) Sand is to
   - bucket ☐
   - castle ☐
   - beach ☐

   as water is to
   - paddle ☐
   - sea ☐
   - cold ☐

3) Car is to
   - road ☐
   - fast ☐
   - wheels ☐

   as train is to
   - long ☐
   - track ☐
   - station ☐

4) Beetle is to
   - insect ☐
   - garden ☐
   - small ☐

   as pigeon is to
   - bird ☐
   - fly ☐
   - seed ☐

5) Ice is to
   - slippery ☐
   - cold ☐
   - wet ☐

   as fire is to
   - red ☐
   - flame ☐
   - hot ☐

6) Turret is to
   - castle ☐
   - flag ☐
   - knight ☐

   as chimney is to
   - smoke ☐
   - house ☐
   - soot ☐

7) Leaf is to
   - crisp ☐
   - tree ☐
   - fall ☐

   as petal is to
   - flower ☐
   - pink ☐
   - garden ☐

8) River is to
   - wet ☐
   - blue ☐
   - water ☐

   as desert is to
   - cactus ☐
   - dry ☐
   - oasis ☐

9) Hat is to
   - bobble ☐
   - cover ☐
   - head ☐

   as glove is to
   - hand ☐
   - warm ☐
   - wool ☐

10) Honey is to
   - sticky ☐
   - bees ☐
   - sweet ☐

   as vinegar is to
   - chips ☐
   - sour ☐
   - bottle ☐

23

1)   E

2)   T

3)   Y

4)   K

5)   H

6)   M

7)   W

8)   R

9)   O

10)   B

1)	R	I	D	**E**	D	I	T	T	A	K	**E**	V	I	L
2)	B	O	L	**T**	R	A	M	M	E	L	**T**	U	R	N
3)	C	O	P	**Y**	E	A	R	O	N	L	**Y**	A	R	D
4)	L	U	C	**K**	N	E	W	B	A	N	**K**	I	N	G
5)	H	I	G	**H**	U	G	E	S	U	C	**H**	A	L	F
6)	F	I	L	**M**	O	O	N	F	A	R	**M**	E	A	T
7)	F	L	O	**W**	A	I	T	S	N	O	**W**	I	S	H
8)	T	O	U	**R**	E	N	T	P	A	I	**R**	E	A	D
9)	L	O	G	**O**	K	A	Y	O	N	T	**O**	P	E	N
10)	C	L	U	**B**	O	N	D	B	U	L	**B**	O	O	K

Move a Letter

2ⁿᵈ New Word

1)	_table	hat	able	_that
2)	cha_nt	sad	chat	sa_nd
3)	_bring	all	ring	_ball
4)	co_uld	for	cold	fo_ur
5)	give_n	had	give	ha_nd
6)	c_rave	fog	cave	f_rog
7)	d_rive	tip	dive	t_rip
8)	s_wing	tin	sing	tw_in
9)	lea_rn	pay	lean	p_ray
10)	_along	try	long	tra_y
11)	ho_use	sit	hose	s_uit
12)	s_port	was	sort	was_p
13)	sol_id	pad	sold	pa_id
14)	bea_rd	own	bear	_down
15)	s_hock	owl	sock	_howl

1)   duck

2)   trip

3)   saw

4)   stalk

5)   ball

6)   kind

7)   rest

8)   train

9)   cool

10) break

Sentence

Hidden Word

1) The children wear hat**s and** gloves in winter. → sand

2) The bird**s oft**en made their nests in the tree. → soft

3) The hungry be**ar ch**ose to eat the sweet honey. → arch

4) They whispered the secret p**lan e**xcitedly to each other. → lane

5) The watchful ha**re st**opped and waited in the field. → rest

6) The tea**m ask**ed who would be playing in the game. → mask

7) The full moon cast a deep sha**dow n**earby. → down

8) The tadpole begins to wrigg**le an**d swims away. → lean

9) She went to play in the park with **her d**og. → herd

10) The old dra**gon e**merged from the dark cave. → gone

27

Answer

1) If the code for HOUSE is KRXVH, what does JDUGHQ mean?
   (+ 3)

2) If the code for SHIP is XMNU, what is the code for TRAIN?
   (+5)

3) If the code for GREEN is FQDDM, what does XDKKNV mean?
   (-1)

4) If the code for LION is MHPM, what is the code for BEAR?
   (+1, -1 alternating)

5) If the code for JUMPER is LWORGT, what does VTQWUGTU mean?
   (+2)

6) If the code for THUNDER is QERKABO, what is the code for SUNSHINE?
   (-3)

7) If the code for HAND is LERH, what does JSSX mean?
   (+4)

8) If the code for PENCIL is VKTIOR, what is the code for PAINT?
   (+6)

9) If the code for MOON is OMQL, what does URCP mean?
   (+2, -2 alternating)

10) If the code for CHERRY is EIGSTZ, what is the code for BANANA?
    (+2, +1 alternating)

GARDEN

YWFNS

YELLOW

CDBQ

TROUSERS

PRKPEFKB

FOOT

VGOTZ

STAR

DBPBPB

Answer

1) (bridge, **dam**, road)   (old, young, **age**)   damage

2) (steam, air, **water**)   (**fall**, trip, stumble)   waterfall

3) (**power**, energy, battery)   (more, **less**, equal)   powerless

4) (day, month, **week**)   (cease, finish, **end**)   weekend

5) (there, **is**, are)   (rock, sky, **land**)   island

6) (**sea**, wave, surf)   (mother, daughter, **son**)   season

7) (yes, **no**, maybe)   (**body**, foot, head)   nobody

8) (**rot**, break, age)   (eight, nine, **ten**)   rotten

9) (out, **in**, near)   (fold, **crease**, bend)   increase

10) (trousers, jacket, **suit**)   (sack, box, **case**)   suitcase

Answer

1) tiny, **huge**, round, medium, **enormous**

| huge | enormous |

2) warm, umbrella, **cold**, **freezing**, raining

| cold | freezing |

3) **far**, near, sky, **distant**, mountain

| far | distant |

4) wide, short, **thin**, tall, **narrow**

| thin | narrow |

5) dirty, **wash**, **scrub**, bubbles, water

| wash | scrub |

6) **start**, lose, **begin**, win, race

| start | begin |

7) awake, **sleep**, bed, **snooze**, pyjamas

| sleep | snooze |

8) plate, spoon, **cup**, teapot, **mug**

| cup | mug |

9) **happy**, bored, **joyous**, party, sad

| happy | joyous |

10) sea, wave, **boat**, sail, **yacht**

| boat | yacht |

		Sum	Answer
1)	If A = 7, B = 9, C = 15, D = 16 and E = 14, what is the answer to the sum written as a letter?	E + B - A =	D
2)	If A = 9, B = 11, C = 16, D = 4 and E = 7, what is the answer to the sum written as a letter?	D + C - B =	A
3)	If A = 4, B = 12, C = 9, D = 17 and E = 8, what is the answer to the sum written as a letter?	D - B + A =	C
4)	If A = 6, B = 10, C = 9, D = 7 and E = 11, what is the answer to the sum written as a letter?	E + A - D =	B
5)	If A = 15, B = 6, C = 18, D = 7 and E = 17, what is the answer to the sum written as a letter?	C - D + B =	E
6)	If A = 23, B = 4, C = 16, D = 11 and E = 13, what is the answer to the sum written as a letter?	A + B - C =	D
7)	If A = 17, B = 19, C = 26, D = 31 and E = 12, what is the answer to the sum written as a letter?	D - A + E =	C
8)	If A = 18, B = 43, C = 49, D = 29 and E = 54, what is the answer to the sum written as a letter?	B + D - A =	E
9)	If A = 28, B = 24, C = 9, D = 26 and E = 5, what is the answer to the sum written as a letter?	A - C + E =	B
10)	If A = 18, B = 16, C = 19, D = 20 and E = 17, what is the answer to the sum written as a letter?	C + E - B =	D

Answer

1) (time, **before**, morning)   (**after**, late, waiting)

before   after

2) (pebble, stone, **blunt**)   (soil, **sharp**, beach)

blunt   sharp

3) (smooth, perfect, **even**)   (number, **odd**, unique)

even   odd

4) (**slow**, competition, walk)   (rush, hurry, **fast**)

slow   fast

5) (bottle, **full**, bag)   (**empty**, eaten, meal)

full   empty

6) (**above**, high, ceiling)   (ground, **below**, down)

above   below

7) (enquire, talk, **question**)   (tell, speak, **answer**)

question   answer

8) (**arrival**, holiday, airport)   (home, **departure**, late)

arrival   departure

9) (dream, **asleep**, blanket)   (**awake**, day, school)

awake   asleep

10) (**create**, draw, paint)   (messy, untidy, **destroy**)

create   destroy

Answer

1) The squirrel buried the **acorn** under the **tree**.

   (acorn)   (tree)

2) Have **you** brushed **your** teeth today?

   (you)   (your)

3) The **rough** waves crashed onto the **sandy** shore.

   (rough)   (sandy)

4) She blew out the **candles** on her birthday **cake**.

   (candles)   (cake)

5) The **alarm** clock rang early in the **morning**.

   (alarm)   (morning)

6) The pool is **where** we **wear** our swimming costumes.

   (where)   (wear)

7) The **stars** shone in the night **sky**.

   (stars)   (sky)

8) The **excited** children opened their **Christmas** presents.

   (excited)   (Christmas)

9) When it is cold, **they** put **their** coats on.

   (they)   (their)

10) **Our** favourite colours **are** red and blue.

   (our)   (are)

Answer

1) **_train_**, ship, boat, **_lorry_**, yacht

2) **_elephant_**, fish, shark, dolphin, **_giraffe_**

3) oak, **_daisy_**, willow, **_daffodil_**, birch

4) **_cat_**, pigeon, **_dog_**, parrot, eagle

5) **_horse_**, beetle, ant, **_hamster_**, centipede

6) **_cold_**, hat, gloves, **_snow_**, scarf

7) gale, hurricane, **_sun_**, cyclone, **_rainbow_**

8) **_cry_**, laugh, **_weep_**, chuckle, giggle

9) pencil, **_paper_**, pen, **_notebook_**, biro

10) **_amble_**, rush, hurry, **_saunter_**, dash

train	lorry
elephant	giraffe
daisy	daffodil
cat	dog
horse	hamster
cold	snow
sun	rainbow
cry	weep
paper	notebook
amble	saunter

		juicy ☐		**vegetable** ☑	
1)	Strawberry is to	**fruit** ☑	as carrot is to	ground ☐	
		red ☐		rabbit ☐	
		bucket ☐		paddle ☐	
2)	Sand is to	castle ☐	as water is to	**sea** ☑	
		beach ☑		cold ☐	
		road ☑		long ☐	
3)	Car is to	fast ☐	as train is to	**track** ☑	
		wheels ☐		station ☐	
		insect ☑		**bird** ☑	
4)	Beetle is to	garden ☐	as pigeon is to	fly ☐	
		small ☐		seed ☐	
		slippery ☐		red ☐	
5)	Ice is to	**cold** ☑	as fire is to	flame ☐	
		wet ☐		**hot** ☑	
		castle ☑		smoke ☐	
6)	Turret is to	flag ☐	as chimney is to	**house** ☑	
		knight ☐		soot ☐	
		crisp ☐		**flower** ☑	
7)	Leaf is to	**tree** ☑	as petal is to	pink ☐	
		fall ☐		garden ☐	
		wet ☑		cactus ☐	
8)	River is to	blue ☐	as desert is to	**dry** ☑	
		water ☐		oasis ☐	
		bobble ☐		**hand** ☑	
9)	Hat is to	cover ☐	as glove is to	warm ☐	
		head ☑		wool ☐	
		sticky ☐		chips ☐	
10)	Honey is to	bees ☐	as vinegar is to	**sour** ☑	
		sweet ☑		bottle ☐	

Non-Verbal Reasoning

Which number is not like the others? Mark the right box.

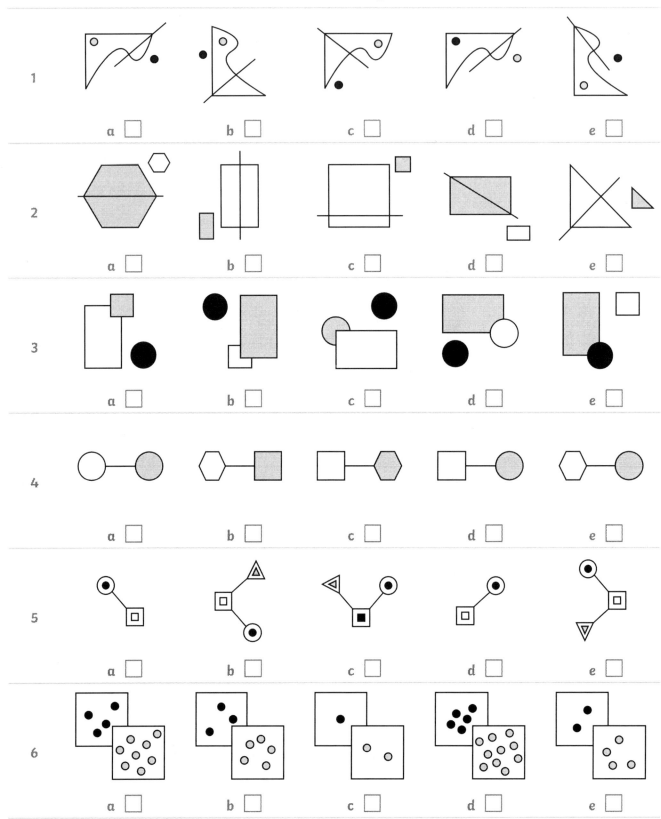

1   a ☐   b ☐   c ☐   d ☐   e ☐

2   a ☐   b ☐   c ☐   d ☐   e ☐

3   a ☐   b ☐   c ☐   d ☐   e ☐

4   a ☐   b ☐   c ☐   d ☐   e ☐

5   a ☐   b ☐   c ☐   d ☐   e ☐

6   a ☐   b ☐   c ☐   d ☐   e ☐

Watch how the first figure changes into the second one.

Mark the shape that the third shape will take on if it is changed the same way.

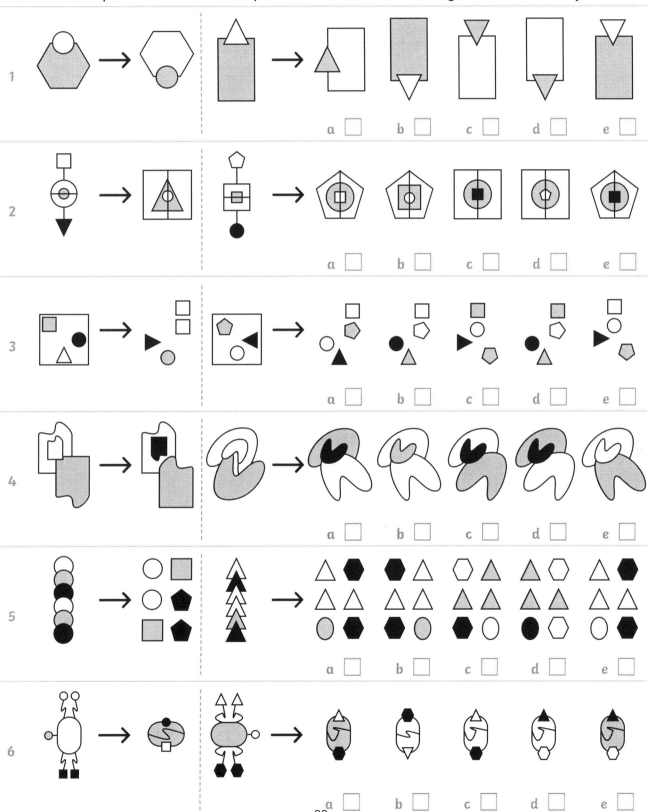

Not a single figure is in any of these sequences. Mark the picture that isn't there.

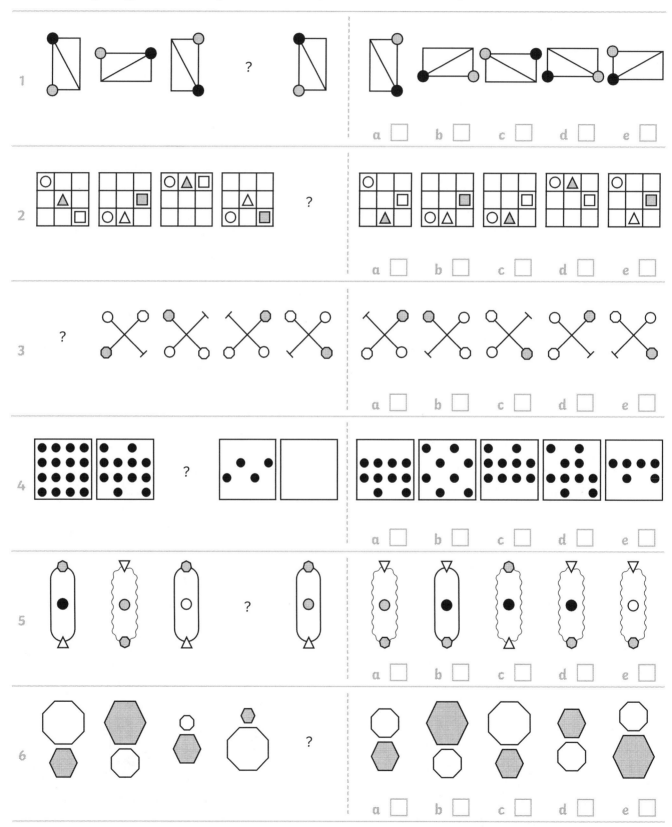

There are three figures on the left in each question that are alike in at least one way. You have to pick the right answer that looks most like the picture on the left.

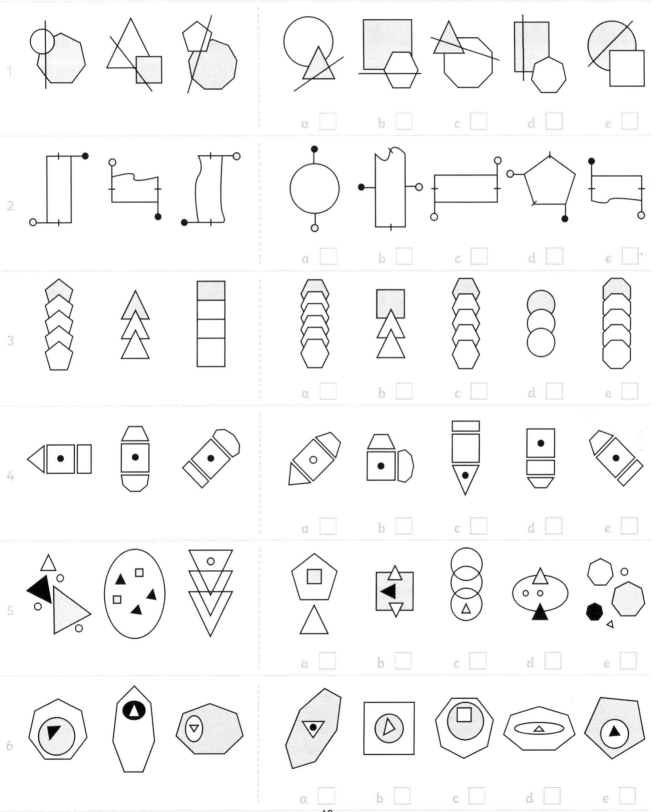

Select the right answer from the list of five that shows the figure on the left. Use the line that says "mirror."

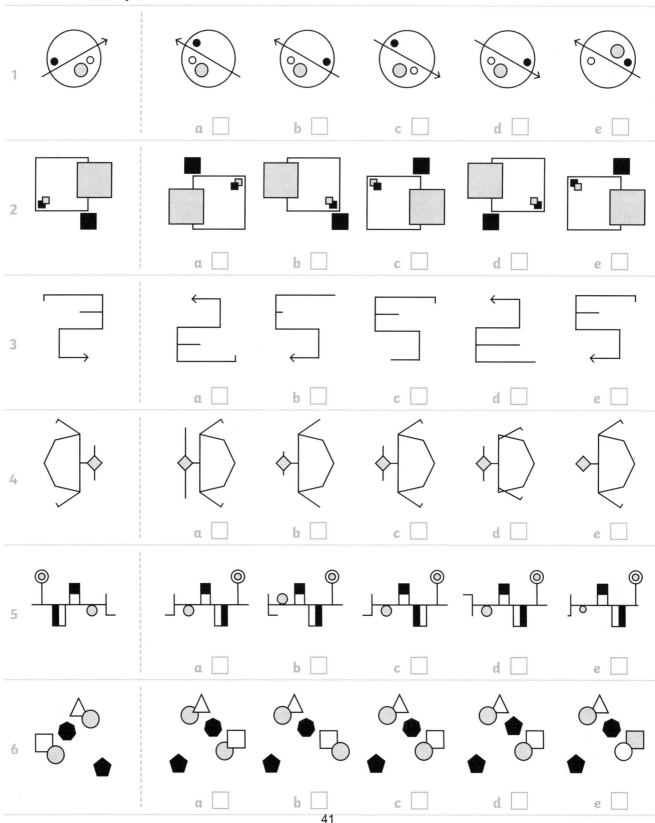

1
a ☐ b ☐ c ☐ d ☐ e ☐

2
a ☐ b ☐ c ☐ d ☐ e ☐

3
a ☐ b ☐ c ☐ d ☐ e ☐

4
a ☐ b ☐ c ☐ d ☐ e ☐

5
a ☐ b ☐ c ☐ d ☐ e ☐

6
a ☐ b ☐ c ☐ d ☐ e ☐

Which square makes the grid whole? Mark the right answer.

1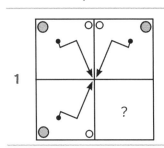

a ☐   b ☐   c ☐   d ☐   e ☐

2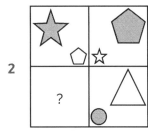

a ☐   b ☐   c ☐   d ☐   e ☐

3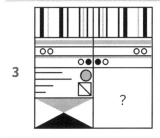

a ☐   b ☐   c ☐   d ☐   e ☐

4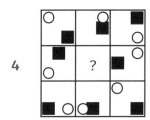

a ☐   b ☐   c ☐   d ☐   e ☐

5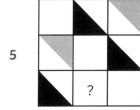

a ☐   b ☐   c ☐   d ☐   e ☐

6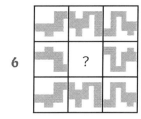

a ☐   b ☐   c ☐   d ☐   e ☐

There are five shapes on the left side of each question. Four of them have a pair of code letters that tell you what they are, but the last shape doesn't have any. Figure out what each letter in the code means, then check off the code that's missing.

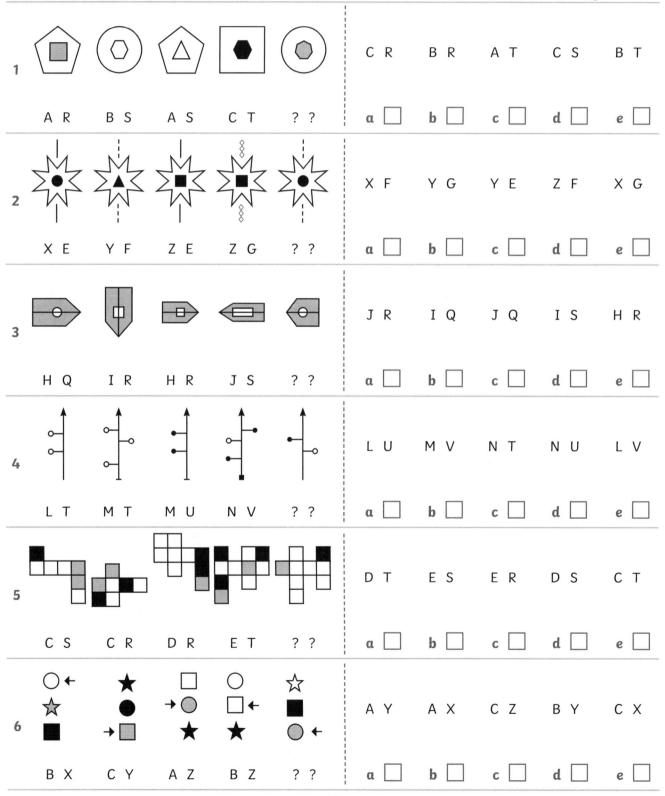

1

C R   B R   A T   C S   B T

a ☐   b ☐   c ☐   d ☐   e ☐

2

X F   Y G   Y E   Z F   X G

a ☐   b ☐   c ☐   d ☐   e ☐

3

J R   I Q   J Q   I S   H R

a ☐   b ☐   c ☐   d ☐   e ☐

4

L U   M V   N T   N U   L V

a ☐   b ☐   c ☐   d ☐   e ☐

5

D T   E S   E R   D S   C T

a ☐   b ☐   c ☐   d ☐   e ☐

6

A Y   A X   C Z   B Y   C X

a ☐   b ☐   c ☐   d ☐   e ☐

Left-side code pairs:

1: A R   B S   A S   C T   ? ?

2: X E   Y F   Z E   Z G   ? ?

3: H Q   I R   H R   J S   ? ?

4: L T   M T   M U   N V   ? ?

5: C S   C R   D R   E T   ? ?

6: B X   C Y   A Z   B Z   ? ?

1　d

In all other figures, the pink circle is inside the shape and the black circle is outside the shape.

2　c

In all other figures, the line divides the larger shape into two equal parts.

3　e

In all other figures, the black circle does not touch any other shape, while the other small shape intersects with the larger shape.

4　a

In all other figures, the two shapes connected by the line are different shapes.

5　c

In all other figures, the smaller square inside the larger square is white.

6　b

In all other figures, the number of black circles are exactly half the number of pink circles.

1   **d**

- The figure has been turned upside down.
- The colours of the shapes have been swapped.

2   **a**

- The top shape in the first figure becomes the largest shape in the second figure.
- The bottom shape becomes the second largest shape and turns orange.
- The small shape in the centre of the middle shape stays the same size but turns white. The middle shape disappears.
- The line that divides the middle shape is turned 90° and now divides the largest shape.

3   **b**

- The three shapes in the box rotate clockwise by 90°.
- The colours of the shapes also rotate - each colour moves clockwise to the next shape.
    - The white shape turns black.
    - The orange shape turns white.
    - The black shape turns orange.
- The outside box shrinks and is placed above the top right shape.

4   **c**

- The orange shape is rotated 180°.
- The smaller white shape is rotated 180° and turns black.

5   **a**

- The white shapes stay the same shape, the orange shapes and the black shapes change into different shapes.
- The shapes are reordered in the following pattern/direction.

6   **d**

- The oval is turned 90°.
- The oval becomes the same colour as the circle that is attached to it with a straight line. This circle and straight line then disappear.
- One of the four wavy lines is rotated 90° and now divides the oval. The other three wavy lines disappear.
- One of the top shapes is brought down to the top of the oval and turns from white to black. The spare top shape disappears.
- One of the bottom shapes is brought up to the bottom of the oval and turns from black to white. The spare bottom shape disappears.

1 b

- The figure rotates 90° clockwise each time.

2 a

- The circle moves between the top and bottom of the shape each time.
- The triangle moves downwards and changes colour each time.
- The square moves upwards and changes colour each time.

3 e

- The line with the coloured circle and white circle on the ends rotates 90° clockwise each time.
- The line with the white circle and the smaller line on the ends rotates 90° anti-clockwise each time.

4 b

- 4 of the circles disappear each time.

5 d

- The triangle and the heptagon move 180° around the oval each time.
- The circle changes colour from black, to gold, to white, and then repeats this pattern.
- The outline of the oval changes between a solid line and a wavy line each time.

6 a

- The hexagon and the octagon switch positions each time.
- The octagon switches from its largest size to its middle size, then to its smallest size, and then jumps back to its largest size and repeats the sequence.
- The hexagon switches from its middle size to its largest size, then back to its middle size, then to its smallest size, and then back to its middle size. It never jumps from largest to smallest, or from smallest to largest.

1   *c*

In all three figures:
- The line intersects both shapes.

2   *e*

In all three figures:
- There is a green circle and a black circle.
- The main shape has four sides.
- The circles connect to the corners of the main shape.

3   *a*

In all three figures:
- The shapes are all the same.
- The total number of shapes correspond to the number of sides of this shape.

4   *e*

In all three figures:
- The square is in the centre of the shapes.
- There is a black circle in the centre of the square.
- The two additional shapes are on opposite sides of the square.

5   *b*

In all three figures:
- There are three triangles.

6   *d*

In all three figures:
- The largest shape has seven sides.
- The second-largest shape has no straight sides.
- The smallest shape is a triangle.

1   b

2   d

3   e

4   c

5   a

6   c

1   *a*

The right column of the grid is a reflection of the left column, using the central vertical line as a mirror line.

The bottom row of the grid is a reflection of the top row, using the central horizontal line as a mirror line.

2   *b*

In each row, the right column of the grid switches the sizes of the shapes in the left column.

The right column is also a mirror reflection of the left column, using the central vertical line as a mirror line.

The colours of the shapes are switched in each row (e.g., in the first row the largest shape is purple and the smaller shape is white, but in the second row the largest shape is white and the smaller shape is purple).

3   *d*

The right column is a mirror reflection of the left column, using the central vertical line as a mirror line.

4   *c*

Looking at each row of the grid from left to right, the white shape moves clockwise around the corners of each box and the black shape moves anticlockwise around the edge of each box.

5   *a*

Looking at each row of the grid from left to right, each box moves one space right each time.

6   *e*

Each row is the same as the row above but flipped vertically.

1   b

A = Larger shape is a pentagon.   B = Larger shape is a circle.   C = Larger shape is a square.

R = Smaller shape is purple.   S = Smaller shape is white.   T = Smaller shape is black.

2   a

X = Inner shape is a circle.   Y = Inner shape is a triangle.   Z = Inner shape is a square.

E = Solid lines.   F = Dotted lines.   G = Diamond patterned lines.

3   c

H = Arrow shape points right.   I = Arrow shape points down.   J = Arrow shape points left.

Q = Inner shape is a circle.   R = Inner shape is a square.   S = Inner shape is a rectangle.

4   e

L = Arrow with nothing on its base.   M = Arrow with line on its base.   N = Arrow with square on its base.

T = All white circles.   U = All black circles.   V = Black and white circles.

5   d

C = 7 squares total.   D = 9 squares total.   E = 10 squares total.

R = 2 black squares.   S = 1 black square.   T = 3 black squares.

6   a

A = Circle is purple.   B = Circle is white.   C = Circle is black.

X = Arrow is on top.   Y = Arrow is on bottom.   Z = Arrow is in the middle.

Non-Verbal Reasoning Part 2

him   big   rabbit

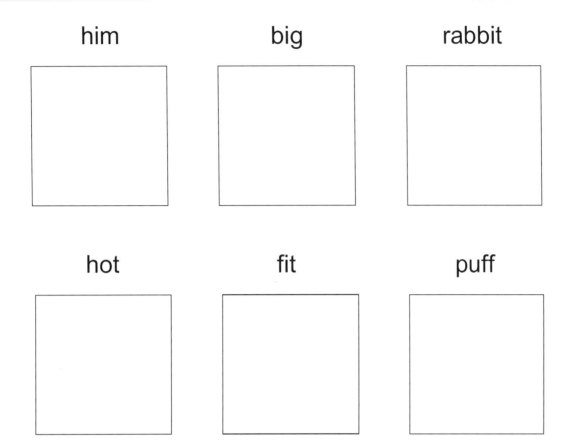

hot   fit   puff

Read the words and match the picture to the word.

his	back	bell

fin	fan	leg

Read the words and match the picture to the word.

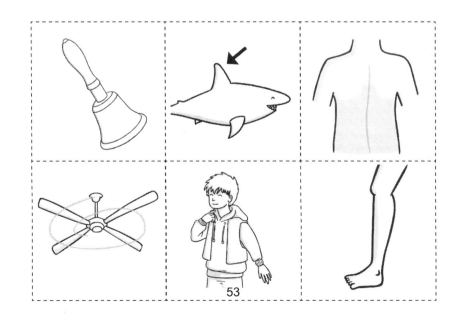

hop   bad   fun

cuff   lit   fill

Read the words and match the picture to the word.

hit

bag

fog

sell

doll

tell

Read the words and match the picture to the word.

55

hut

bed

bucket

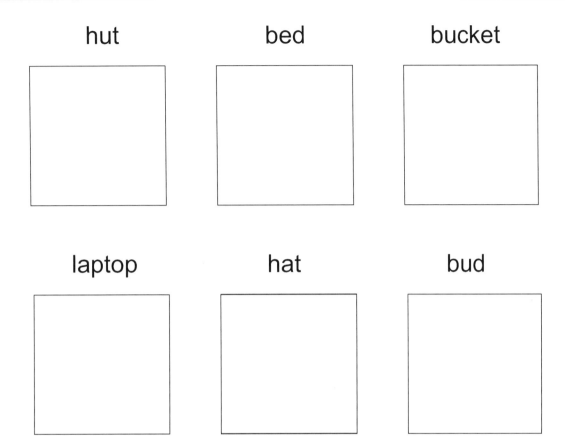

laptop

hat

bud

Read the words and match the picture to the word.

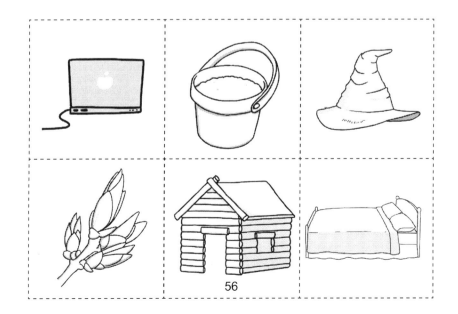

56

hug

bug

bun

fig

hiss

boss

Read the words and match the picture to the word.

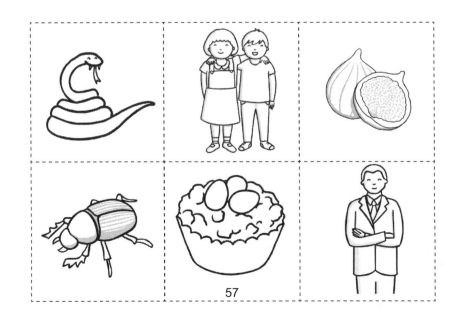

bus   bit   bat

mess   kiss   pass

Read the words and match the picture to the word.

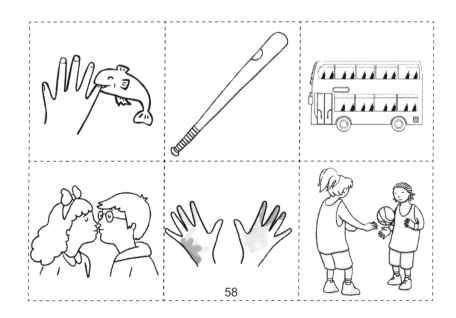

58

huff   fat   beg

lap   grass   off

Read the words and match the picture to the word.

sit

nip

pan

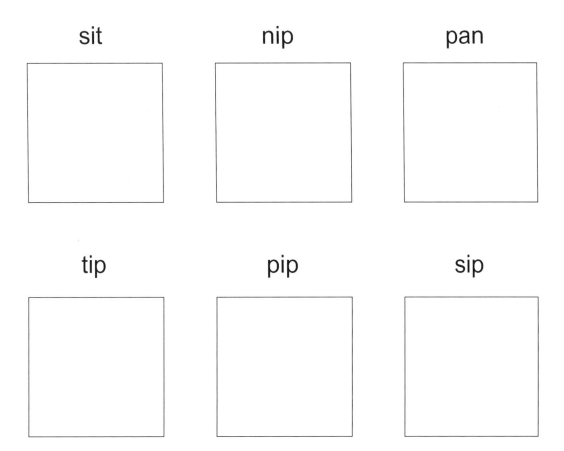

tip

pip

sip

Read the words and match the picture to the word.

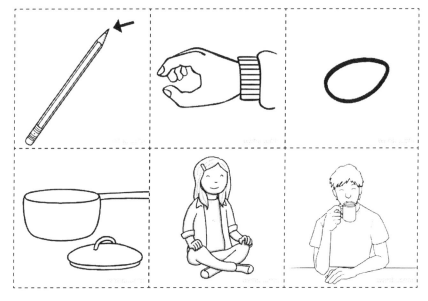

pin	sat	tin

tan	nap	man

Read the words and match the picture to the word.

mat   map   dad

pit   dip   sad

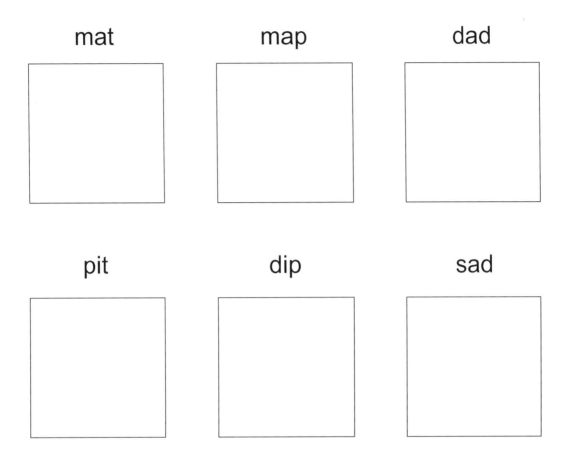

Read the words and match the picture to the word.

tag

pot

gap

dig

gas

pig

Read the words and match the picture to the word.

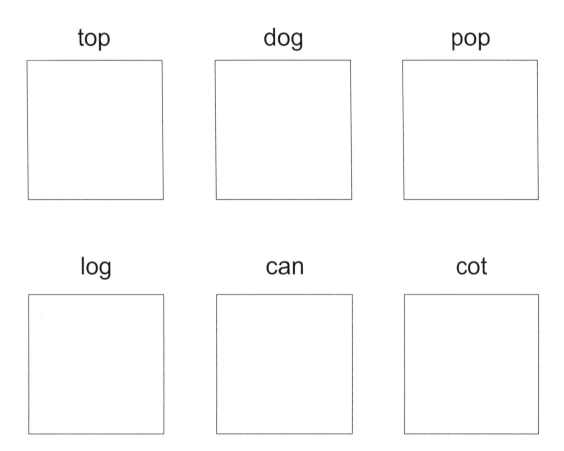

Read the words and match the picture to the word.

cop

cap

cat

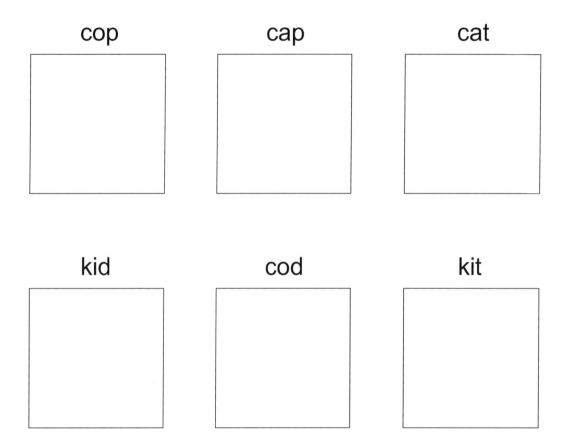

kid

cod

kit

Read the words and match the picture to the word.

kick

sock

sack

pick

sick

pack

Read the words and match the picture to the word.

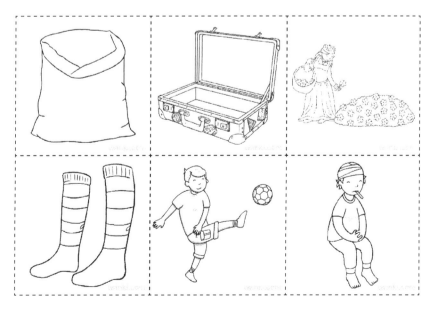

ticket

pocket

pet

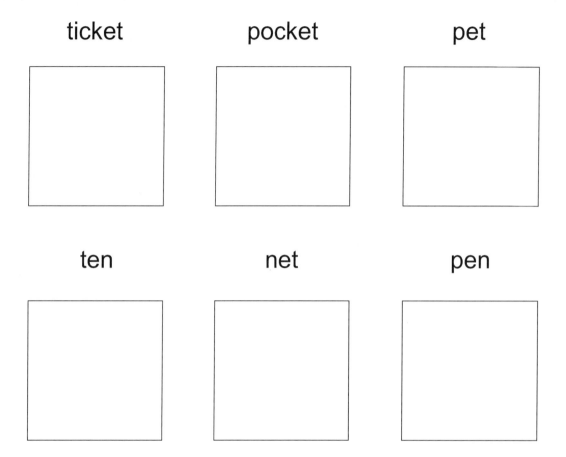

ten

net

pen

Read the words and match the picture to the word.

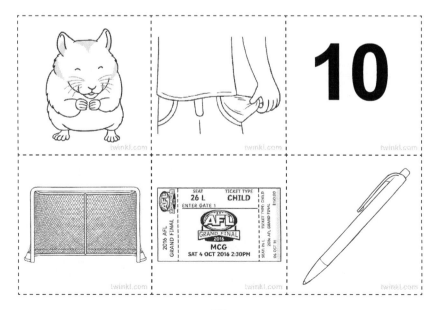

peg

men

neck

up

mum

run

Read the words and match the picture to the word.

mug	rip	sun

mud	sunset	ram

Read the words and match the picture to the word.

rat

rag

cup

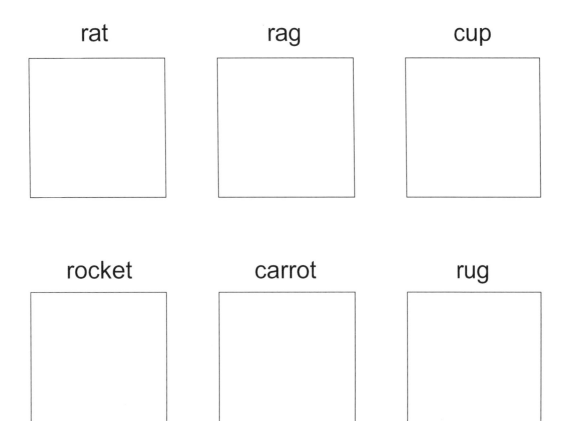

rocket

carrot

rug

Read the words and match the picture to the word.

Explore other books from the Serie:

Canada
Amazon Store:

US
Amazon Store:

Explore Other books by Mirvoxid Press

Score Higher, Achieve More with Mirvoxid Press

these and more other Test Preps and Study Guides on Amazon Store:

Canada Store:

US Store:

Made in United States
Troutdale, OR
12/22/2024

27074966R00042